KEN LENNOX
TUPPENCE STONE

Dear Reader

This little book might look to you just like a little book, but it's actually a Little Miracle. A year ago we asked the legendary Delia to help us do something for Comic Relief – she suggested giving us her next recipe collection. As her last collection had done fairly well (bestselling hardback of all time ever, ever, ever, apart from the Bible), we had to hug and kiss her a lot and refer to her always as St Delia.

The next thing we knew, her husband Michael (are saints allowed to marry?) agreed to publish these 12 five-minute recipes in a £1 book without charging a penny. Then Delia met the head of Birds Eye Wall's. Nobody knows what she said, but suddenly Birds Eye Wall's agreed to sponsor *all the costs involved* in making the book. (Birds Eye Wall's instantly became our best friends in the whole world and we all started eating a lot of frozen peas so they knew how grateful we were.)

In November 1996, Dawn and I, Angus Deayton, Jennifer Saunders and Gary '2.4 Tummies' Olsen each made a five-minute programme with Delia to demonstrate the recipes, and then Sainsbury's, WHSmith, Savacentre, Wellworths and Menzies all agreed to sell three million of our books and not make any profit at all.

Finally – and this is the best bit – you bought this copy, and for doing that, we love every inch of you, even the inches other people avoid. So now there's only one more thing you can do for us. Turn to page 17 and have a big think about using the recipes to do a fundraising event for Comic Relief. That would be the icing on the mini-muffin.

We in turn promise to spend your money wisely and really make a difference to the projects we support across the UK – homeless people on the streets of London, young disabled people, pensioners living below the poverty line in Glasgow, teenagers whose lives are being destroyed by drugs and alcohol in Liverpool and thousands of people fighting for a fair chance of life throughout Africa.

In the past decade we've raised over £112 million. Because all our fundraising costs are sponsored, this means that we have spent over £112 million directly on projects. I've visited a lot of them over the years, and I've seen things that would break your heart – and things that would make you very proud indeed that you've helped us.

A big thank-you to you – eat, eat and then have some pudding.

Lenny Henry

SMALL CHANGE
BIG
DIFFERENCE
**RED NOSE DAY
MARCH 14TH '97**

CRUMPET PIZZAS
Serves 4 as a snack, or 2 as a main course

Well, it does make sense if you think about it – soft, squidgy bread that gets lightly toasted for just a bit of crunch, then all those wonderful holes so that the cheese and other ingredients can melt right down into it. And because crumpets are quite small, the fillings get piled up very high and it all becomes rather lovely!

I have four versions on offer here, but you can get really creative and make up loads more ideas of your own. Obviously, the whole thing can also be very easily adapted to whatever happens to be available.

First be sure to preheat the grill, because it needs to be really hot – so give it a good 10 minutes. Then all you do is lightly toast the crumpets on each side (they can be quite close to the heat at this stage) – you need for them to be lightly golden, which takes about 1 minute on each side. Then remove them to a baking sheet and quickly pile on the topping ingredients. Then back they go under the hot grill, but this time 5in (13cm) from the heat source. Each of the versions will take exactly 5 minutes to mingle, melt and bubble, then you can serve them absolutely immediately.

The classic four seasons pizza

4 crumpets, toasted

1 rounded tablespoon sundried tomato paste

3oz (75g) mozzarella, cut into small cubes

2 small open mushrooms, thinly sliced

4 slices prosciutto, chopped

1 tablespoon salted capers, rinsed

4 cherry tomatoes, thinly sliced

4 anchovy fillets, drained and sliced through the centre

4 pitted black olives

4 basil leaves, torn

1 tablespoon olive oil

Preheat the grill to its highest setting.

I didn't initially believe I could get this amount of topping on crumpets, but I did, and so can you. First spread each toasted crumpet with sundried tomato paste, then put the cubes of mozzarella over each pizza. Then, in your mind, imagine four quarters and put the sliced mushrooms on one quarter of each crumpet, the chopped prosciutto on another, the capers on the third quarter, and finally the sliced tomato. Now lay the anchovies over in a criss-cross pattern, which will divide the quarters. Then add the olives and the torn basil leaves. Finally, drizzle a few drops of olive oil over everything and grill, as described above, for 5 minutes.

The Sophisticat's pizza

4 crumpets, toasted

6oz (175g) gorgonzola, cubed

2oz (50g) chopped walnuts

2oz (50g) mozzarella, cubed

12 medium sage leaves

1 tablespoon olive oil

This pizza is for sophisticated foodies: equally simple but a little bit posher than the other versions. All you do is scatter the gorgonzola over each crumpet, then sprinkle with the chopped walnuts, then the cubes of mozzarella and finally place the sage leaves – first dipped in the olive oil – on top. Then drizzle a few more drops of the olive oil over and grill as above for 5 minutes, by which time the cheese will have melted, the walnuts toasted and the sage become crisp.

American hot pizza

4 crumpets, toasted

6oz (175g) fontina, gruyère or mozzarella, grated

2 hot pepperami, thinly sliced

2 red chillies, seeds left in, thinly sliced

1 heaped tablespoon salted capers, rinsed

2 teaspoons chopped fresh oregano

2 red chillies, seeds left in, halved lengthways

1 tablespoon olive oil

These pizzas can be fiery hot and quite macho, so if you like them 'mop-your-brow' hot you can add more chilli, otherwise the quantities here will give you a little bit of heat but really more of a spicy kick! Put half the cheese on the crumpets, then scatter the pepperami and thinly sliced chillies all over. Then follow this with the rest of the cheese, capers and oregano and top with half a chilli. Lastly, sprinkle on a few drops of olive oil and grill for 5 minutes, as above.

Keep it simple

(Pizza for kids)

4 crumpets, toasted

1 rounded tablespoon sundried tomato paste

5oz (150g) cheddar, grated

4 slices ham, Parma ham or salami, chopped

2 small open mushrooms, thinly sliced

4 cherry tomatoes, sliced thinly

1oz (25g) parmesan, freshly grated

4 basil leaves, torn

4 cherry tomatoes, stalk left on

1 tablespoon olive oil

This version is for very young people who don't like too much fancy stuff. It's basically cheddar cheese, ham and tomato, but we tried it with salami instead of ham and all our young

friends seemed to like that, too. First spread the crumpets with the sundried tomato paste, then sprinkle the cheese over the crumpets and pat it down with the palm of your hand. Next arrange the ham (or salami) all over the cheese, then cover that with the sliced mushrooms on one half and sliced tomatoes on the other. Now sprinkle on some parmesan cheese and the torn basil, then place a whole cherry tomato on top, stalk and all, but prick it first with a fork to stop it from popping. Drizzle a little olive oil over the tomato and place the pizza under the grill and cook, as above, for 5 minutes.

The classic four seasons pizza

The Sophisticat's pizza

American hot pizza

Keep it simple

Bloody Mary soup

BLOODY MARY SOUP
Serves 2

More of a Virgin Mary really, but there's nothing to stop you adding a shot of vodka if you have the mind to. Honestly, though, it won't need it because it has a lovely spicy kick of its own, and the very best news is it must easily be the fastest soup on record, although it tastes as though it took hours!

3 ripe tomatoes, weighing 6oz (175g)
1 x 18fl oz (510ml) carton fresh tomato juice
1 tablespoon Worcestershire sauce
1 tablespoon balsamic vinegar
juice of 1 lime
4 drops Tabasco sauce
salt and freshly milled black pepper

To garnish
celery salt
2 rounded dessertspoons crème fraîche
a few sprigs watercress

First put the kettle on, then place the tomatoes in a bowl, pour boiling water over them and count 30 seconds. After that, pour off the water and slip off the skins. Now chop the tomatoes very finely, then add the whole lot to a medium-sized saucepan. Bring the tomatoes up to a gentle simmer and let them cook for about 3 minutes. Next, pour in the tomato juice and the rest of the ingredients and season with salt and pepper. Do a bit of tasting here – it might need a dash more Tabasco or another squeeze of lime. Now bring everything back up to simmering point, then ladle the soup into warm soup bowls straight away. Quickly swirl in a rounded dessertspoon of crème fraîche into each one. Then add a few sprigs of water-cress, a generous sprinkling of celery salt and serve with the warm goat's cheese, onion and potato bread.

GOAT'S CHEESE, ONION AND POTATO BREAD
Serves 4-6

Don't make this if you are on a diet – it's so wonderful it's impossible to stop eating it. It's also great for a packed lunch or a journey because you've got the bread and cheese all in one! It must also be the quickest, easiest homemade bread on record.

4oz (110g) firm goat's cheese, peeled and cut into
small cubes
4-5 spring onions, finely sliced

1 medium red potato, weighing approx 6oz (175g)
6oz (175g) self-raising flour
1 level teaspoon salt
pinch cayenne
1 rounded teaspoon chopped thyme leaves
1 large egg
2 tablespoons milk
1 rounded teaspoon grain mustard
a little flour for dusting

You will also need a baking sheet, very well greased.
Preheat the oven to gas mark 5, 375°F, 190°C.

Start off by peeling the potato and grating it on the coarse side of the grater straight into a big, roomy mixing bowl. Now sift in the flour, salt and cayenne, holding the sieve up high to give the flour a good airing. Next in go the spring onions, thyme and two-thirds of the cheese. Then take a palette knife and blend everything together thoroughly.
After that beat the egg gently with the milk and mustard, then pour the mixture into the bowl, just bringing it all together to a loose rough dough, still using the palette knife. Next transfer it on to the baking sheet and pat it gently into a 6in (15cm) rough round. Now lightly press the rest of the cheese over the surface, dust with a little flour and bake the bread on the middle shelf of the oven for 40-45 minutes or until it is golden brown. Then remove it to a cooling tray and serve it still slightly warm from the oven if possible (but I have to say it's still divine a day later).

Goat's cheese, onion and potato bread

7

A SOUFFLE OMELETTE
WITH THREE CHEESES AND CHIVES
Serves 1

Though making a soufflé proper can be a stressful experience, particularly if you've had no practice, making a soufflé omelette is a doddle. It takes no more than 5 minutes and honestly tastes every bit as good as the oven-baked variety. This one has three cheeses, but you can make it with just one, or even four if you happen to have them hanging around. Served with the sweet-and-sour red onion salad, it's probably one of the nicest and quickest meals for one person I know.

3 large eggs
1 heaped tablespoon finely snipped chives
½oz (10g) butter
1oz (25g) parmesan, finely grated
1oz (25g) strong cheddar, finely grated
1oz (25g) gruyère, finely grated
salt and freshly milled black pepper

You will also need a medium solid-based frying pan with a base diameter measurement of 7in (18cm).
Preheat the grill to its highest setting for 10 minutes and have a warm plate ready.

First separate the eggs – yolks into a small bowl and whites into a squeaky-clean large bowl; it helps if you separate the whites singly into a cup first before adding them to the bowl, then if one breaks, it won't ruin the rest. Now beat the egg yolks with a fork, seasoning well with salt and pepper. Next put the pan on to a low heat to warm through. While that's happening, whisk the egg whites with either an electric hand whisk or a balloon whisk, until they form soft peaks. Next add the butter to the pan and turn the heat up. Then, using a large metal spoon, quickly fold the egg yolks into the egg whites, adding the cheddar, half the parmesan and the chives at the same time. Then, when the butter is foaming, pile the whole lot into the pan and give it a good hefty shake to even it out. Now let the omelette cook for 1 minute exactly. Then slide a palette knife round the edges to loosen it, sprinkle the grated gruyère cheese all over the surface and whack the omelette under the grill, about 4in (10cm) from the heat. Now let it cook for 1 more minute, until the cheese is melted and tinged golden. Next remove the pan, then slide the palette knife round the edge again, take the pan to the plate then ease one half of the omelette over the other and tilt the whole lot out on to the plate. Then scatter the rest of the parmesan all over and serve immediately.
Note If you want to make this omelette for 2, that's okay if you double everything. Just use a 9 or 10in (23 or 25.5cm) pan and give each stage more time, then divide the omelette into halves.

Sweet and sour red onion salad

SWEET AND SOUR RED ONION SALAD
Serves 1

This is a great accompaniment to the soufflé omelette. It can be served warm or at room temperature, and once you have tried it you will realise how well it goes with lots of other things, particularly bangers and mash!

1 medium red onion, cut into 8 wedges through the root
1 tablespoon olive oil
1 rounded teaspoon light soft brown sugar
1 tablespoon water
1 tablespoon red wine vinegar
1 rounded teaspoon grain mustard
salt and freshly milled black pepper

All you do is heat the oil in a small saucepan, add the onion and turn the heat down to low and let it cook gently for 5 minutes, stirring now and then. Next add the sugar and water, stir well then pop the lid on and let it continue cooking gently for another 10 minutes. After that add the vinegar and mustard and a seasoning of salt and pepper, give everything another really good stir then turn the heat out while you make the soufflé omelette. Then serve the salad with it.

**Soufflé omelette
with three cheeses and chives**

Chocolate drop mini-muffins with red noses

Coffee fudge bananas with toasted nuts

CHOCOLATE DROP MINI-MUFFINS
WITH RED NOSES
Makes 24

Tiny little chocolate bites – soft, light, with melted chocolate swirled on the top, on which to fix a whole cherry. Once you've mastered the very easy art of making these, you simply have to make at least 100 – if not more. Then once you and the family have eaten all you can, sell the rest to your friends and send the profits to Comic Relief (details on page 17).

5oz (150g) plain flour
2 level tablespoons cocoa powder
1 level dessertspoon baking powder
¼ teaspoon salt
1 large egg, lightly beaten
1½oz (40g) golden caster sugar
4fl oz (120ml) milk
2oz (50g) butter, melted and cooled slightly
2oz (50g) plain chocolate drops

For the topping
2¾oz (65g) plain chocolate drops
24 red glacé cherries
icing sugar, sifted

You will also need 2 x 12-hole mini-muffin tins, well greased.

Preheat the oven to gas mark 6, 400°F, 200°C.

Start off by sifting the flour, cocoa powder, baking powder and salt into a large bowl. Then in a separate bowl mix together the egg, sugar, milk and melted butter. Now return the dry ingredients to the sieve and sift them straight on to the egg mixture (this double sifting is essential because there won't be much mixing going on). What you need to do now is take a large spoon and fold the dry ingredients into the wet ones – quickly, in about 15 seconds. Don't be tempted to beat or stir, and don't be alarmed by the rather unattractive, uneven appearance of the mixture: this, in fact, is what will ensure that the muffins stay light. Now fold the chocolate drops into the mixture – again with a minimum of stirring; just a quick folding in.

Divide the mixture between the muffin cups, about 1 heaped teaspoon in each, and bake on a high shelf in the preheated oven for 10 minutes, until well risen. Then remove the muffins from the oven and cool in the tins for 5 minutes before transferring them to a cooling tray.

While they're cooling, place the remaining chocolate drops into a small bowl. Then place this into a saucepan of barely simmering water without allowing the bowl to touch the water, and allow the chocolate to melt. Then, when the muffins are cool enough to handle, spoon a little melted chocolate on to each one, then place it back on the cooling tray and fix a cherry on top. If you like, before serving you can give them a dusting of sifted icing sugar.

COFFEE FUDGE BANANAS
WITH TOASTED NUTS
Serves 4

The world record for making this recipe is not five minutes, but only three. It's quite simply the fastest dessert recipe I've ever come across. It's also amazingly good and if it is conceivable that anybody on this earth does not love the delectably thick Greek yogurt, then you can make it just as well with whipped cream.

2 large ripe bananas
1 x 500g tub Greek yogurt
5oz (150g) unrefined molasses sugar
2 level teaspoons instant coffee powder
2oz (50g) Brazil nuts

You will also need 4 individual dessert glasses of 7fl oz (200ml) capacity.

Preheat the grill to its highest setting.

Right, on your marks, get ready...Pop the Brazil nuts spread out on some foil under the grill about 4in (10cm) from the heat and put a timer on for 3 minutes (if you haven't got a timer keep an eye on them, because they will burn if you forget them).
Now peel and slice the bananas into thin rounds. Place them in a large bowl then add the yogurt and mix well. Now divide the mixture between 4 individual glasses. Mix the sugar thoroughly with the coffee powder and simply sprinkle this equally over the 4 portions of banana. Now cover with clingfilm and leave in the fridge for about 3 hours. Then remove the nuts from the grill as soon as they're toasted and keep them on one side for later.
By the time 3 hours have passed the sugar and coffee mixture will have transformed itself into lovely pools of fudge sauce. So now all you need to do is to chop the nuts, sprinkle them on top, serve and wait for the compliments.

Very red rice

OVEN-BAKED CHICKEN IN MAPLE BARBECUE SAUCE
Serves 4

Yes, it's really true: although the chicken does take about 50 minutes to cook, the actual work involved takes no more than 5 minutes.

4 chicken thighs and 4 drumsticks, or a chicken jointed into 8
1 tablespoon olive oil
1 dessertspoon lemon juice
1 medium onion, chopped small
salt and freshly milled black pepper

For the sauce
3fl oz (75ml) red wine
4 tablespoons Japanese soy sauce
2 tablespoons red wine vinegar
1 heaped tablespoon tomato purée
2 tablespoons pure maple syrup
1 heaped teaspoon ground ginger
1 heaped teaspoon mustard powder
2 cloves garlic, peeled and crushed
1½ teaspoons Tabasco sauce

To finish
2fl oz (55ml) red wine
a few sprigs watercress

You will also need a shallow roasting tin, measuring 12 x 8 x 1¾in (30 x 20 x 4.5cm)

First of all mix the olive oil with the lemon juice, then place the chicken joints in a roasting tin with the chopped onion tucked amongst them. Season with a little salt and freshly milled black pepper and brush the oil and lemon juice all over everything. You can, if you like, do this well in advance, cover with a cloth and leave in a cool place.
When you're ready to cook the chicken, preheat the oven to gas mark 6, 400°F, 200°C, then pop the chicken in on a high shelf and let it cook for 25 minutes exactly. Meanwhile, combine all the sauce ingredients in a jug and, using a small whisk, blend everything thoroughly. Then, when the 25 minutes are up, remove the chicken from the oven, pour off any surplus fat from the corner of the tin, then pour the sauce all over, giving everything a good coating.

Now back it goes into the oven for about another 25 minutes (you will need to baste it twice during this time). After that, remove the roasting tin from the oven and place it over direct heat turned to medium. Then pour in the extra 2fl oz (55ml) of red wine, stir it into the sauce, let it just bubble for about 1 minute, then serve the chicken with the sauce spooned over. Garnish with a few sprigs of watercress and some very red rice alongside.

VERY RED RICE
Serves 4

For certain reasons (which by now you must know about) I've increased the 'red' content of this recipe, so red pepper and red onion are combined with red rice, which make it very seductive, especially if you serve it with the oven-baked chicken.

10fl oz (275ml) red rice
15fl oz (425ml) boiling water
1 small red onion, finely chopped
1 small red pepper, deseeded and finely chopped
1 level teaspoon salt
1 tablespoon oil
½oz (10g) butter

To serve
2 spring onions, finely sliced

The best way to cook any rice is in a frying pan with a lid. So first find a lid that fits a large frying pan and start off by heating the oil and butter over a medium heat. Then turn it up to high and stir-fry the chopped pepper and onion until they are softened and slightly blackened at the edges – about 6-7 minutes. After that turn the heat right down, add the red rice to the pan and stir it round to get a good coating of oil. Now pour in the boiling water and salt, and stir again. When it reaches simmering point put the lid on and let it cook very gently for 40 minutes. After that, don't take the lid off, just turn the heat out and leave it for another 15 minutes to finish off. Then serve the rice garnished with some sliced spring onions sprinkled over.

Oven-baked chicken
in maple barbecue sauce

THE RED NSE SUPPER PARTY PLAN

MENU

Bloody Mary soup
Goat's cheese, onion and potato bread

Oven-baked chicken in maple barbecue sauce
Very red rice

Coffee fudge bananas with toasted nuts

If you want to give a supper party for your friends, I've tried to make it easier for you by working out a time plan. This won't keep you occupied all the time, but it will enable you to waft through it all without any worry. And in between you'll have time to have a shower, set the table, pour yourself an aperitif and clear up as you go...

5pm First switch the grill on. Then prepare the coffee fudge bananas, cover and place them in the fridge. After that grill the nuts, but *please* don't leave them or they might burn!

5.15pm Now prepare the first stage of the chicken, cover with a cloth and leave it in a cool place. Then mix all the sauce ingredients in a jug and keep it aside till later.

5.45pm You now need to switch on the oven to gas mark 5, 375°F, 190°C, and then make the bread.

6pm Now the bread goes into the oven for 40-45 minutes. Meanwhile you can set the table, prepare the ingredients for the rice, make the Bloody Mary soup and leave it ready in a pan to reheat.

6.20pm Take a break till...

6.45pm Take the bread out of the oven and turn the heat up to gas mark 6, 400°F, 200°C.

6.50pm Pop the chicken into the oven on the highest shelf, then put the rice on to cook.

7pm If you like, you can now take a shower or listen to *The Archers*.

7.15pm Now hike the chicken out of the oven, drain off the fat, pour the sauce over and pop it back into the oven.

7.25pm Baste the chicken.

7.30pm Turn the heat out under the rice and leave it still covered.

7.35pm Baste the chicken again.

7.40pm Now the chicken is ready. Turn the oven off and take the chicken out. Then pop the bread back in to warm, along with the plates and serving dishes.

7.50pm Dinner is served! Don't forget to garnish the soup with crème fraîche, watercress and celery salt. Don't forget to put the spring onions on the rice.

And please, please don't forget to pass the hat round for **COMIC RELIEF**

THE
FOOD FUNDRAISING
FORM

Dear Friend of Foodie,

The person who has just waved this piece of paper under your nose is raising money for Comic Relief by organising a culinary caper. In recognition of their excellent effort, all you have to do is sponsor them. It's as simple as Gary Rhodes.

A million lightly toasted thank-yous.

I agree to sponsor (name) ....

who is preparing to (event) ....

	ABSOLUTELY, UTTERLY & COMPLETELY FABULOUS PROMISER'S NAME	AMOUNT PER...	TOTAL RECEIVED	PROMISER'S INITIALS
THE GORGEOUS MR(S)				
THE DIVINE MR(S)				
THE SUCCULENT MR(S)				
THE DELICIOUS MR(S)				
THE HALF-BAKED MR(S)				
THE TASTY MR(S)				
THE SLIGHTLY BURNT MR(S)				
THE PARBOILED MR(S)				
THE NICE-SMELLING MR(S)				
THE OVERSTUFFED MR(S)				
THE SAUCY MR(S)				
THE FAT-FREE MR(S)				
THE CALORIFIC MR(S)				
THE SPICY MR(S)				
THE FRANKLY RATHER DISGUSTING DESPITE ALL THE EFFORT MR(S)				
OH COME ON, PUT THE ICING ON THE CAKE!				

TOTAL RAISED £ _____

Name ....

Address ....

....

Postcode .... Tel ....

....

Total amount enclosed ....

Signed ....

Parent/guardian if under 18 ....

Please return this form with your payment to

**KPMG
PO BOX 678
LONDON EC4Y 8AS**

Cheque/postal orders should be crossed and made payable to 'Comic Relief 97 Red Nose Collection'. PLEASE DON'T SEND CASH THROUGH THE POST • ONLY RETURN THIS FORM AFTER YOUR EVENT Comic Relief is a registered charity, number 326568.

See overleaf for ideas on how to raise lots of money for Comic Relief ➤

HOW TO TURN YOUR COOKER INTO A CASH-MAKER

Now you know how to make fabulous food in five minutes, what we want you to cook up is a recipe that makes money as well. Here we suggest a smorgasbord of ideas to help. And our guarantee is that for every single penny you raise, a penny will go directly to helping the very poorest people both in Africa and here in the UK.

Breakfast
Why not turn your house into a B & B? For one morning only, charge everyone for breakfast (double if they want it in bed!).

Mid-morning
Make a big round of chocolate drop mini-muffins with red noses and sell them to your classmates or colleagues. Make tea for everyone and charge them for delivery to their desk.

Lunch
If you have kids, why not get them to prepare lunch for you? Then get them to serve you as if you were in a restaurant. The bill you pay can then go to Comic Relief. Or make them an extra special packed lunch every day of the week and deduct it from their pocket money.

Tea
Throw a tea party and charge your guests a tiny price for every tiny slice of cake, or every muffin they eat. It all adds up. Remember: small change, big difference!

Supper
Have a Comic Relief Supper Party (see page 16) and charge your guests £1 per course. Make them pay extra for additional vodka shots in their Bloody Mary soup. And then get them to tip for your excellent service. Encourage your guests to tell jokes while you are eating, and one quid to you whenever they crack shockingly old gags.

On the night of Comic Relief
On 14 March on BBC1, we're promising you six hours of the best comedy we can make. Why don't you charge your household for the ultimate TV dinner? Or make a huge pile of muffins and sell them for 20p each. Or crumpet pizzas at 50p each.

Whatever you do, use the sponsorship form in this booklet to make it as simple as possible, have as much fun as you can and send the money you raise (however little it may be) to us. Even your small change will make a big difference to the crucial work we support. We love you for taking part in this.

£1 buys a simple home delivery kit for an Ethiopian midwife, which will help prevent mothers and babies suffering infection during childbirth.

JUST £1.70 pays for the cost of a Ghanaian women to attend a literacy course.

JUST 50p pays for a drugs and alcohol information booklet for young people in the UK.

£1.25 pays for a cooked breakfast for a young homeless person in a night shelter.

LEGAL DOs AND DON'Ts

Be safe. Don't do anything illegal or dangerous. And get permission for your event.

On all your publicity, including fundraising materials and press releases, you must state that 'Comic Relief is a registered charity, no 326568'.

Take care not to involve children under 16 in collecting sponsorship money. Make sure children never approach strangers.

Tell the local press what you are up to and spread the word.

Obvious, but find a responsible person to pay the money you raise into any bank or building society or post office.

Make sure you don't collect with buckets in the street. The only house-to-house collections you can do are when you're collecting your sponsorship money from friends and relatives.